FEB 1 7 2011

S0-CFU-113

Pebble® Plus

First Ladies

Martha Washington

by Sally Lee

Consulting Editor: Gail Saunders-Smith, PhD

Consultant: Carl Sferrazza Anthony, Historian
National First Ladies' Library
Canton, Ohio

CAPSTONE PRESS
a capstone imprint

Pebble Plus is published by Capstone Press,
151 Good Counsel Drive, P.O. Box 669, Mankato, Minnesota 56002.
www.capstonepub.com

Copyright © 2011 by Capstone Press, a Capstone imprint. All rights reserved.
No part of this publication may be reproduced in whole or in part, or stored in a retrieval system, or transmitted in any
form or by any means, electronic, mechanical, photocopying, recording, or otherwise, without written permission of the
publisher. For information regarding permission, write to Capstone Press,
151 Good Counsel Drive, P.O. Box 669, Dept. R, Mankato, Minnesota 56002.
Printed in the United States of America in North Mankato, Minnesota.

032010
005740CGF10

 Books published by Capstone Press are manufactured with paper
containing at least 10 percent post-consumer waste.

Library of Congress Cataloging-in-Publication Data
Lee, Sally.
Martha Washington / by Sally Lee.
p. cm.—(Pebble plus. First Ladies)
Summary: "Simple text and photographs describe the life of Martha Washington"—Provided by publisher.
Includes bibliographical references and index.
ISBN 978-1-4296-5011-3 (library binding)
ISBN 978-1-4296-5605-4 (paperback)
1. Washington, Martha, 1731–1802—Juvenile literature. 2. Presidents' spouses—United States—Biography—Juvenile
literature. I. Title. II. Series.
E312.19.W34L44 2011
973.4'1092—dc22   2009053409

Editorial Credits
Christine Peterson, editor; Ashlee Suker, designer; Svetlana Zhurkin, media researcher; Eric Manske,
    production specialist

Photo Credits
Art Resource, N.Y./The New York Public Library, 16–17
The Bridgeman Art Library/Virginia Historical Society, Richmond, Virginia, 9
Corbis/Bettmann, 1, 12–13, 21
Getty Images/Stock Montage, cover (right); SuperStock, 18–19
The Granger Collection, New York, 6–7
Library of Congress, 10–11, 15
Line of Battle Enterprise, 5
Shutterstock/Alaettin Yildirim, 5, 7, 9, 11, 13, 15, 21 (caption plate); antoninaart, cover (left), 1, 5–6, 8–9, 20–21, 22–23,
    24 (pattern); Gemenacom, 9, 21 (frame); Mikhail Olykainen, 5 (frame)

Note to Parents and Teachers

The First Ladies series supports national history standards related to people and culture. This
book describes and illustrates the life of Martha Washington. The images support early readers
in understanding the text. The repetition of words and phrases helps early readers learn new
words. This book also introduces early readers to subject-specific vocabulary words, which are
defined in the Glossary section. Early readers may need assistance to read some words and to
use the Table of Contents, Glossary, Read More, Internet Sites, and Index sections of the book.

Table of Contents

Early Years

Martha Washington

was known for her kindness.

The future first lady was born

June 2, 1731, in Virginia.

Martha was the oldest

of John and Frances

Dandridge's eight children.

born in
Virginia

1731

young Martha
Washington

3 0053 00936 4640

5

Martha didn't go to school.

Instead she learned

how to run a home.

Martha's mother taught her

to spin wool, cook, and sew.

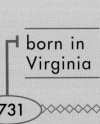

born in
Virginia

1731

Martha was born at this Virginia home.

Family Life

In 1750 Martha married

Daniel Custis.

They had four children,

but two died as babies.

Daniel died in 1757.

Martha was left alone

with two small children.

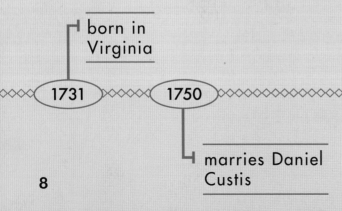

born in
Virginia

1731   1750

marries Daniel
Custis

Martha's two children, John (left) and Martha (right)

In 1759 Martha married

George Washington.

They moved to George's

Virginia plantation

called Mount Vernon.

Martha was in charge of

the workers and farm goods.

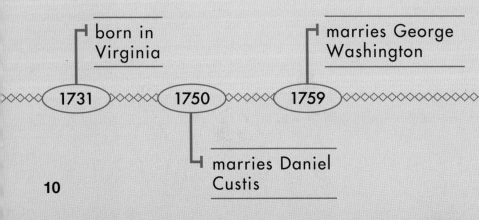

born in
Virginia

marries George
Washington

1731   1750   1759

marries Daniel
Custis

George and Martha Washington at their wedding, 1759

The War

In 1775 the American colonies

went to war against

Great Britain. George led

the American army.

Martha joined him at his

army camp every winter.

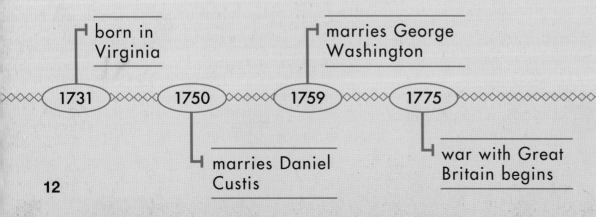

born in
Virginia

marries George
Washington

1731   1750   1759   1775

marries Daniel
Custis

war with Great
Britain begins

12

Martha (far right) visited troops during the war.

Martha wanted to help

the ragged soldiers.

She visited the sick men.

Martha knitted warm socks

and made them clothes.

She wrote letters to raise

money for food and clothes.

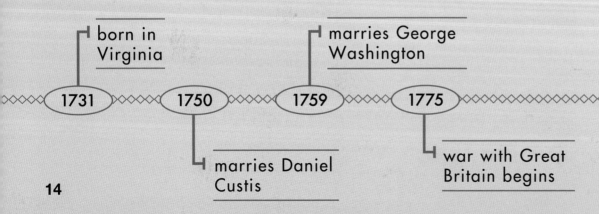

born in
Virginia

marries George
Washington

1731   1750   1759   1775

marries Daniel
Custis

war with Great
Britain begins

Martha (center) knitted socks for soldiers.

First Lady

The colonies won the war.

In 1789 George became

the first U.S. president.

Martha became first lady.

She wanted a quiet life.

But Martha knew the country

needed George.

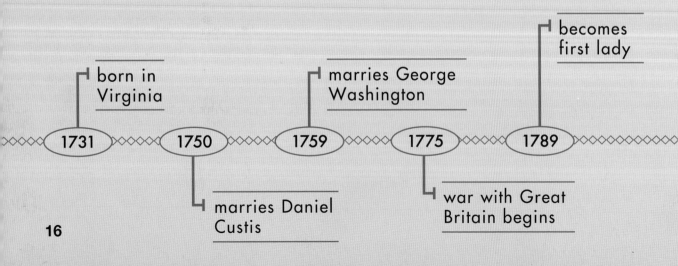

born in
Virginia

marries George
Washington

becomes
first lady

1731 — 1750 — 1759 — 1775 — 1789

marries Daniel
Custis

war with Great
Britain begins

As first lady, Martha gave

dinner parties.

She held weekly teas

for the public.

Her kindness made people

feel welcome. People called her

Lady Washington.

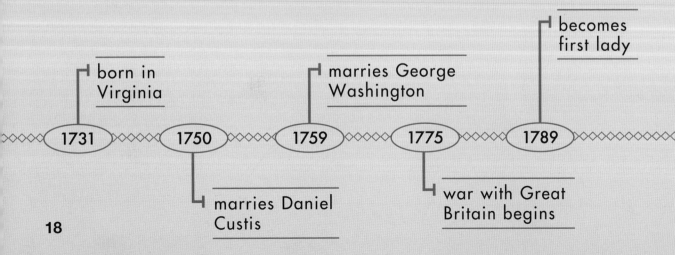

becomes
first lady

born in
Virginia

marries George
Washington

1731 — 1750 — 1759 — 1775 — 1789

marries Daniel
Custis

war with Great
Britain begins

19

George was president

for eight years.

He died in 1799.

Martha was too sad

to go to his funeral.

In 1802 Martha died

at age 70.

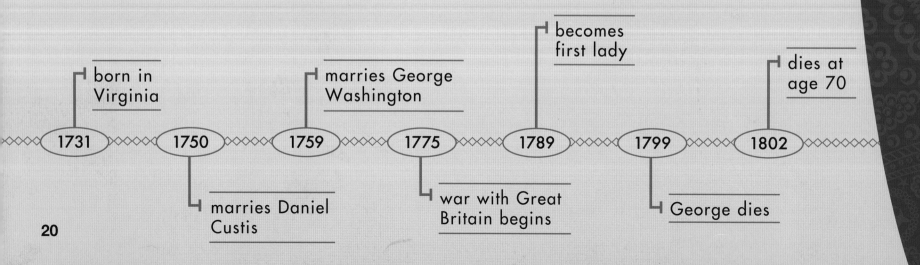

born in
Virginia

marries George
Washington

becomes
first lady

dies at
age 70

1731   1750   1759   1775   1789   1799   1802

marries Daniel
Custis

war with Great
Britain begins

George dies

portrait of Martha painted late in her life

Glossary

colony—an area settled by people from another country and ruled by that country; the 13 American colonies were controlled by Great Britain

funeral—a ceremony for a person who has died

plantation—a large farm that grows crops like coffee, tea, and cotton

ragged—tired or worn out

spin—to make thread by twisting together thin fibers

tea—a social gathering at which tea and other foods are served

wool—the soft, thick, curly hair of sheep or goats; wool is used to make yarn and fabric

Read more

Mayer, Cassie. *George Washington*. First Biographies. Chicago: Heinemann Library, 2008.

Slade, Suzanne. *Martha Washington: First Lady of the United States*. Biographies. Minneapolis: Picture Window Books, 2008.

Internet Sites

FactHound offers a safe, fun way to find Internet sites related to this book. All of the sites on FactHound have been researched by our staff.

Here's all you do:

Visit *www.facthound.com*

FactHound will fetch the best sites for you!

Index

Word Count: 239
Grade: 1
Early-Intervention Level: 22